The Journey of Light

From Promise to Fulfillment in Christ

30-Day Christmas Devotional

THE JOURNEY OF LIGHT
From Promise to Fulfillment in Christ
30-Day Christmas Devotional

Cover design and interior layout: Nadia A. L. Farrington & Hendia Minnis
Edited and published by: Haeli Minnis & Nadia Farrington
www.whispersatsunrise.com

ISBN: 979-8-9930641-3-0
Printed in the United States of America

May this devotional be a light to every heart that seeks Him the fulfillment of promise found in Christ alone.

Dedication

I dedicate this devotional to my mother a woman whose unwavering love mirrors the heart of God.

Through every season, she has shown me what it means to trust Him fully, to pray without ceasing, and to stand firm in faith when life's storms arise. Her quiet strength, her steadfast prayers, and her unshakable belief have been a guiding light for all who know her.

She has encouraged her children to walk in purpose and consistently shown her daughters what it means to be women of faith anchored in grace, clothed in humility, and radiant with hope. Her life is a living testimony that trusting God is never in vain.

For every lesson, every prayer, and every example of love this devotional is a reflection of the light she's helped kindle within me.

Acknowledgment

I give all glory and honor to God, the true Author of every word written within these pages. Without His light, there would be no story to tell. His presence has guided me through every chapter, reminding me that all things find their purpose in Him.

To my family thank you for your love, patience, and encouragement throughout this journey. Your prayers, understanding, and faith have been a constant source of strength.

To my friends and supporters those who have spoken words of life, shared kind encouragement, or simply believed in what God has placed in me your support means more than words can express.

To every reader who has opened this devotional thank you for allowing me to share this journey of faith and light with you. May these pages draw you nearer to the heart of Christ and renew your wonder of His presence.

Above all, I acknowledge the Holy Spirit, whose gentle whispers and guidance made this devotional possible. May *The Journey of Light* be a vessel that points every heart back to Him.

Table of Contents

Table of Contents

Preface

Every story of redemption begins with light breaking through darkness. From the first promise spoken in Genesis to the cry heard in Bethlehem, Scripture tells of a faithful God who fulfills His word in His perfect time. *The Journey of Light* was written to help you walk through that story day by day until the miracle of Christmas becomes more than a season, but a living revelation of Christ within you.

This devotional is an invitation to slow down and remember what Advent truly means: longing for the Savior, welcoming His presence, and reflecting His glory in our lives. Each day's reading draws from the promises, prophecies, and fulfillment found in Jesus Christ the Word made flesh.

As you journey through these pages, may the light that once filled the manger fill your heart anew. May hope rise where weariness once lived, and may every promise remind you that God's faithfulness still shines in the waiting.

My prayer is that by the end of these 30 days, you will see Christmas not just as a date on the calendar, but as the continual story of Emmanuel God with us dwelling in every moment of your life.

Introduction

The Journey of Light: From Promise to Fulfillment in Christ is more than a Christmas devotional it's an invitation to rediscover the wonder of God's promises fulfilled in Christ. Each page leads you through the unfolding story of redemption, from the first glimmer of hope in Scripture to the radiant light that entered the world in Bethlehem.

Throughout these 30 days, you'll walk through the anticipation of a Savior long-awaited, the miracle of His arrival, and the eternal hope His presence brings. This devotional is designed to quiet the noise of the season and turn your focus toward the heart of Christmas Emmanuel, God with us.

Every reading includes Scripture, reflection, and truth meant to draw you nearer to the Light of the world. Whether read in the stillness of the morning or by candlelight at the end of the day, may these moments remind you that the story of Christmas is not confined to a manger but continues in every heart that welcomes Him.

As you move from promise to fulfillment, may faith rise within you. May the same light that pierced the darkness over two thousand years ago shine anew in your life today. And may your journey through these pages leave you standing in awe of the One who came near, who still dwells among us, and who will one day return in glory.

How To Use This Devotional

This 30-day devotional is designed to help you draw nearer to Christ through Scripture, reflection, and prayer as you journey from promise to fulfillment. Each day invites you to slow down and *dwell in the Word* to linger in the light of God's truth and listen for His voice.

Begin with prayer

Ask the Holy Spirit to open your heart and mind to the truth of God's Word. Invite Him to speak personally through each passage and reflection.

"Open thou mine eyes, that I may behold wondrous things out of thy law." — Psalm 119:18

Scripture

Begin by reading the main passage for the day.
Pause and allow the Word to settle in your heart before moving on.

"Thy word is a lamp unto my feet, and a light unto my path." — Psalm 119:105

Dwelling in the Word

This section replaces the traditional "Devotional Reading." Here you'll find a short reflection designed to help you linger in God's truth seeing His character, promises, and light revealed through each verse.

"Open thou mine eyes, that I may behold wondrous things out of thy law." — Psalm 119:18

Supportive Scriptures to Reflect

These additional passages deepen your time in the Word. Read them slowly and prayerfully, allowing Scripture to interpret Scripture. They are meant to strengthen your understanding and stir your faith.

"Let the word of Christ dwell in you richly in all wisdom." — Colossians 3:16

Prayer

Conclude your reading by speaking with God from the heart. Thank Him for His faithfulness, confess where you need His light, and invite His truth to take root in you.

"Continue in prayer and watch in the same with thanksgiving." — Colossians 4:2

Reflection Questions

Use this space to write what the Holy Spirit is revealing to you. Reflect honestly and personally your answers become part of your journey.

"But be ye doers of the word, and not hearers only." — James 1:22

Each page is an opportunity to pause, listen, and respond. As you move through these 30 days, may the Word become living light in your heart guiding you from promise to fulfillment, and from reflection to transformation.

Longing For A Savior

Before the manger, before the star, there was a deep and holy longing. Humanity had walked in darkness, waiting for the promised Redeemer who would bring light to the world. Generation after generation looked toward heaven with hope that God's Word would be fulfilled that the Messiah would come to heal, restore, and reign in righteousness.

In these first ten devotions, we journey through the ancient promises and prophetic glimpses that stirred this anticipation. Each passage reflects the yearning of hearts that awaited Emmanuel God with us. As you read, allow your own heart to awaken with that same expectancy. Let every verse remind you that even in seasons of waiting, God is faithful to His Word, and His promises are always fulfilled in Christ.

ONE

The Promise in the Garden

Genesis 3:15 *And I will put enmity between thee and the woman, and between thy seed and her seed; it shall bruise thy head, and thou shalt bruise his heel.*

Dwelling in the Word

The story of Christmas does not begin in Bethlehem, but in the Garden of Eden. When Adam and Eve chose to disobey God, sin entered the world, and with it came death, shame, and separation from the Creator. Humanity lost the peace of walking with God in the cool of the day. Yet even in that moment of failure, God spoke a word of hope.

In Genesis 3:15, often called the protoevangelium (the first gospel), the Lord declared that a Redeemer would come the seed of the woman who would crush the serpent's head. The enemy of our souls would wound Him, but ultimate victory would belong to the promised Savior.

This first promise whispers of Jesus. Though the serpent sought to destroy, God already had a plan of redemption. Jesus, born of a woman, entered our broken world to destroy the works of the devil (**1 John 3:8 KJV** *He that committeth sin is of the devil; for the devil sinned from the beginning. For this purpose the Son of God was manifested, that he might destroy the works of the devil.*) The manger, the cross, and the empty tomb were not afterthoughts but the fulfillment of God's ancient promise.

As we begin this devotional journey toward Christmas, we are reminded that the celebration of Christ's birth is not merely about a baby wrapped in swaddling clothes it is about God's faithfulness through the ages. Long before shepherds heard angels sing, long before wise men brought gifts, God's heart was set on redemption. God has given us countless promises that lead to His plans for us. Galatians 4:4-5 KJV reminds us that He will send forth His Son made of a woman to redeem us that we might receive adoption of sonship. ***"but when the fulness of the time was come, God sent forth his Son, made of a woman, made under the law, to redeem them that were under the law, that we might receive the adoption of sons."***

The Christmas story begins with a promise. And that promise assures us that no failure is final, no darkness too deep, and no sin too strong for the Savior who was to come.

God's promises never fail. What He has spoken will come to pass in His perfect time. Even when the wait feels long, His Word remains sure. Trust His timing every promise is a reminder that God is faithful from beginning to end.

Supporting Scriptures

Romans 16:20 *And the God of peace shall bruise Satan under your feet shortly. The grace of our Lord Jesus Christ be with you. Amen.* (Connects to the fulfillment of the serpent's defeat through Christ.)

Isaiah 7:14 *Therefore the Lord himself shall give you a sign; Behold, a virgin shall conceive, and bear a son, and shall call his name Immanuel.* (Prophetic echo of the "seed of the woman.")

Prayer

Lord, thank You for being a God of promise and redemption. From the very beginning, You planned a way to restore what was broken. As I walk through these next 30 days, prepare my heart to see Jesus not just as a baby in Bethlehem, but as the promised Savior who conquers sin and death. Help me to rest in Your faithfulness today. Amen.

Reflection Question

Where in your life do you need to be reminded that God's promises are stronger than the enemy's lies?

TWO

The Blessing Through Abraham

Genesis 22:18 *And in thy seed shall all the nations of the earth be blessed; because thou hast obeyed my voice.*

Dwelling in the Word

God's plan of redemption continued through His covenant with Abraham. After Abraham's willingness to offer up Isaac, God reaffirmed His promise: through Abraham's seed, all the nations of the earth would be blessed.

This blessing pointed beyond Abraham's descendants to Jesus Christ, the ultimate Seed (**Galatians 3:16** *Now to Abraham and his seed were the promises made. He saith not, And to seeds, as of many; but as of one, And to thy seed, which is Christ.*) The birth of Jesus is the fulfillment of God's global promise, a Savior not only for Israel but for the whole world. Christmas is the celebration of a gift that extends to every tribe, tongue, and nation.

The beauty of this promise is that it rests not on human ability but on God's faithfulness. Abraham believed God, even when the path was unclear. In the same way, we are called to trust that His promises are true, even when life's circumstances test us. The birth of Jesus is proof that God keeps His word, no matter how impossible it may seem.

When we look at the manger, we are seeing God's covenant love stretched across generations. The star over Bethlehem shone for shepherds and kings alike a light for all people. And today, you are included in that blessing.

God's blessings are already on the path He's called you to walk. Stay focused, keep your eyes on Him, and don't be distracted by what hasn't happened yet. What God has for you will come in His time just keep moving forward in faith.

Supporting Scriptures

Genesis 12:2-3 *And I will make of thee a great nation, and I will bless thee, and make thy name great; and thou shalt be a blessing: and I will bless them that bless thee and curse him that curse thee: and in thee shall all families of the earth be blessed.* **(The original covenant promise that is later reaffirmed in Genesis 22.)**

Romans 4:13 *For the promise, that he should be the heir of the world, was not to Abraham, or to his seed, through the law, but through the righteousness of faith.* **(Reveals the covenant's true nature fulfilled by faith, not law.)**

Prayer

Father, thank You for fulfilling Your covenant promises through Jesus Christ. Thank You that Your blessing extends beyond boundaries, reaching every nation including me. Help me to live as one who has received Your blessing, and to share it with others. Amen.

Reflection Question

How does knowing that you are part of God's promise to bless the nations change the way you see your role in the world today?

Through Abraham's blessing, God opened the door for His grace to reach every nation and every heart willing to believe.

THREE

The Scepter Shall Not Depart

Genesis 49:10 *The sceptre shall not depart from Judah, nor a lawgiver from between his feet, until Shiloh come; and unto him shall the gathering of the people be.*

Dwelling in the Word

In Jacob's blessing over his sons, a prophetic word was spoken to Judah: the scepter, a symbol of kingship and authority, would remain in his line until Shiloh came. "Shiloh" is understood by many to point to the Messiah the One who would bring peace and gather the people to Himself.

Centuries later, Jesus was born in the line of Judah, the rightful heir to David's throne, fulfilling this ancient promise. The manger held not only a child but a King, the King of kings who would rule with righteousness and peace.

Christmas reminds us that Jesus is not only Savior but Sovereign. The baby in Bethlehem is also the Lion of Judah. His kingdom is not fragile or passing, but everlasting. While earthly rulers rise and fall, His throne endures forever.

Luke 1:32-33 *He shall be great and shall be called the Son of the Highest: and the Lord God shall give unto him the throne of his father David: And he shall reign over the house of Jacob forever; and of his kingdom there shall be no end.*

As we prepare our hearts in this season, we must ask: have we allowed Him to reign in our lives? The true joy of Christmas is found not only in His coming but in His kingship bringing order, peace, and hope to our hearts. Let your heart rest in His peace, be lifted by His hope, and overflow with His joy. Jesus reigns our King who rules with love and faithfulness. No matter what comes, His Kingdom stands, and so does your victory in Him.

Supporting Scriptures

Numbers 24:17 *I shall see him, but not now: I shall behold him, but not nigh: there shall come a Star out of Jacob, and a Sceptre shall rise out of Israel, and shall smite the corners of Moab, and destroy all the children of Sheth.* (Another prophetic image of a coming ruler fulfilled in Christ.)

Revelation 5:5 *And one of the elders saith unto me, Weep not: behold, the Lion of the tribe of Judah, the Root of David, hath prevailed to open the book, and to loose the seven seals thereof.* (Christ's eternal kingship fully revealed in heaven.)

Prayer

Lord Jesus, thank You for being both my Savior and my King. Help me to surrender every area of my life to Your rule. This Christmas, may I not only celebrate Your birth but also welcome Your reign in my heart. Amen.

Reflection Question

What area of your life needs to come under the kingship of Christ this season?

When we dwell in the Word, the Word begins to dwell in us shaping our thoughts, strengthening our faith, and guiding our steps.

FOUR

A Prophet Like Moses

***Deuteronomy 18:15** The LORD thy God will raise up unto thee a Prophet from the midst of thee, of thy brethren, like unto me; unto him ye shall hearken.*

Dwelling in the Word

Before Israel entered the Promised Land, Moses told the people that God would raise up another Prophet like him one who would speak God's Word with authority. This was not merely another leader; it was a foreshadowing of Christ, the ultimate Prophet who reveals the heart and will of God perfectly.

Moses was a deliverer, a lawgiver, and an intercessor. Yet he was only a shadow of what Jesus would be. Christ came as the greater Deliverer, leading us out of bondage to sin; the greater Lawgiver, writing God's truth on our hearts; and the greater Intercessor, forever standing before the Father on our behalf.

Christmas reminds us that God did not leave us in silence. He spoke fully through His Son **(Hebrews 1:1–2)**. Every word Jesus spoke carried life, truth, and freedom. Today, He still calls us to listen, to obey, and to follow His voice above all others.

Jesus came to give us life that overflows, truth that sets us free, and freedom that no one can take away. When you walk with Him, you walk in light, purpose, and unshakable hope.

Supportive Scriptures

Acts 7:37 *This is that Moses, which said unto the children of Israel, A prophet shall the Lord your God raise up unto you of your brethren, like unto me; him shall ye hear.* **(Stephen reaffirms that this prophecy pointed to Jesus.)**

John 6:14 *Then those men, when they had seen the miracle that Jesus did, said, This is of a truth that prophet that should come into the world.* **(Crowds understood the connection between Jesus' miracles and Moses' words.)**

Prayer

Lord Jesus, You are the greater Prophet, revealing the Father's heart to us. Help me to listen carefully to Your voice and obey Your Word. Teach me to follow You faithfully this season. Amen.

Reflection Question

Whose voice has the loudest influence in your life right now and how can you give more attention to the voice of Christ?

True peace is found when we listen to the voice of Jesus and obey without delay.

FIVE

A Shoot from Jesse's Stump

Isaiah 11:1 *And there shall come forth a rod out of the stem of Jesse, and a Branch shall grow out of his roots.*

Dwelling in the Word

Isaiah spoke of a day when the royal line of David, which seemed cut down and hopeless, would produce new life. Out of Jesse's stump a symbol of something that looked finished would come a Branch, a new King who would bring righteousness and peace.

This is the story of Christmas. When hope seemed gone, when the royal line was obscured by years of exile and silence, Jesus came as the Branch. His life was evidence that God can bring beauty out of barrenness and life out of what looks dead.

Perhaps you have areas in your life that feel like stumps places cut down, dreams withered, hope nearly gone. Remember, the God who brought forth a Savior from a dead stump can bring renewal to you as well. Christmas is a testimony that no situation is beyond God's power to restore.

Here are a few uplifting examples to encourage your heart.

Broken Dreams Restored

Maybe you've faced closed doors, failed plans, or opportunities that seemed lost. Just as new life sprang from Jesse's stump, God can breathe purpose back into what felt finished. Trust that His "no" may be preparing the ground for a greater "yes."

Hope After Heartbreak

If your heart has been cut down by disappointment or loss, remember God specializes in resurrection. Healing may come slowly, but His love is quietly restoring what pain tried to destroy.

Faith in a Dry Season

You might be in a season where nothing seems to grow your prayers feel unanswered, your faith weary. Yet beneath the surface, God is nurturing roots of promise. Don't give up before the new shoot appears.

Renewal of Purpose

Perhaps you've drifted, unsure of your direction. The birth of Jesus reminds us that God still fulfills His promises, even after long silence. Surrender your plans and let Him bring life to what once seemed lifeless.

Restoration of Joy

If joy feels distant, remember that renewal begins not in circumstances but in surrender. Invite the Lord to renew your spirit; He can turn sorrow into songs of praise.

Supportive Scriptures

Jeremiah 33:15 *In those days, and at that time, will I cause the Branch of righteousness to grow up unto David; and he shall execute judgment and righteousness in the land.* (Echoes Isaiah's vision of a just and holy ruler.)

Romans 15:12 *And again, Esaias saith, There shall be a root of Jesse, and he that shall rise to reign over the Gentiles; in him shall the Gentiles trust.* (Paul quotes Isaiah 11:1 to show that Jesus is the promised Root and King for all nations.)

Prayer

Father, thank You for bringing life where there seemed to be none. Thank You for Jesus, the Branch of Jesse, who brings hope to every weary heart. Renew me this season with Your Spirit. Amen.

Reflection Question

What "stump" in your life do you need to surrender to God so He can bring new growth and hope?

SIX

Born of a Virgin

Isaiah 7:14 *Therefore the Lord himself shall give you a sign; Behold, a virgin shall conceive, and bear a son, and shall call his name Immanuel.*

Dwelling in the Word

Seven hundred years before Jesus' birth, Isaiah prophesied a miraculous sign: a virgin would conceive and bear a son named Immanuel "God with us." This prophecy points directly to the miracle of the Incarnation.

The virgin birth is not a small detail; it is the foundation of our faith. Jesus did not come by the will of man but by the power of God. Fully God and fully man, He entered the world untouched by sin's curse, able to redeem us.

Christmas is more than a sentimental story it is a miracle. God became flesh and dwelt among us. This is why we can never reduce the season to lights, gifts, and traditions alone. At its core, Christmas is about the holy God choosing to step into humanity, to walk with us, and to save us.

Here are a few encouraging reminders that reveal how this truth comes alive in our everyday lives:

God Draws Near in Our Loneliness

When you feel unseen or forgotten, remember that Christmas proves God came close. He didn't stay distant He entered our world, so we'd never walk alone again.

Hope in the Midst of Brokenness

Jesus came into a world filled with pain and sin to bring healing and redemption. Whatever feels broken in your life, He can restore it with His presence and peace.

Light in the Darkness

When life feels dark or uncertain, remember that the Light of the world has come. No darkness is too deep for His love to shine through.

Strength in Our Weakness

God didn't come for the perfect He came for the weary, the lost, and the humble. When you feel weak, His grace meets you there and lifts you up.

Joy That Transcends Circumstances

Because God came to be with us, joy is no longer tied to what's happening around us but Who is within us.

Supportive Scriptures

Matthew 1:22-23 *Now all this was done, that it might be fulfilled which was spoken of the Lord by the prophet, saying. Behold, a virgin shall be with child, and shall bring forth a son, and they shall call his name Emmanuel, which being interpreted is, God with us.* (Direct fulfillment and confirmation that Jesus' birth completed Isaiah's prophecy.)

Luke 2:10-11 *And the angel said unto them, Fear not: for, behold, I bring you good tidings of great joy, which shall be to all people. For unto you is born this day in the city of David a Saviour, which is Christ the Lord.* (The angel's announcement to Mary a supernatural conception by the Holy Spirit.)

Prayer

Immanuel, thank You for entering this world in such a miraculous way. Thank You that You are truly God with us. Help me to stand in awe of the miracle of Your birth and never lose the wonder of Christmas. Amen.

Reflection Question

How does remembering the miracle of the virgin birth deepen your appreciation of God's power and love?

SEVEN

Prince of Peace

Isaiah 9:6 *For unto us a child is born, unto us a son is given: and the government shall be upon his shoulder: and his name shall be called Wonderful, Counsellor, The mighty God, The everlasting Father, The Prince of Peace.*

Dwelling in the Word

Isaiah's prophecy paints a picture of the Messiah's identity. Among His titles is "Prince of Peace." In a world filled with conflict, chaos, and division, the coming of Jesus meant the arrival of peace, peace with God, peace within ourselves, and peace with others.

The peace Christ brings is not simply the absence of war or trouble. It is *shalom* wholeness, completeness, and restoration. At Christmas, the angels declared, "Peace on earth, goodwill toward men" (**Luke 2:14** *Glory to God in the highest, and on earth peace, good will toward men.*) This peace is available to all who receive Him.

Today, many chase peace through possessions, success, or relationships, but true peace can only be found in Christ. He carries the government upon His shoulders, meaning He has the authority to calm storms both around us and within us.

Christmas invites us to rest in His reign and let His peace rule our hearts.

When Christ reigns within us, chaos loses its power. His peace steadies our minds, quiets our fears, and reminds us that He is still in control.

Supportive Scriptures

John 16:33 *These things I have spoken unto you, that in me ye might have peace. In the world ye shall have tribulation: but be of good cheer; I have overcome the world.* (His peace sustains us even amid trouble a hallmark of His reign.)

Philippians 4:7 *And the peace of God, which passes all understanding, shall keep your hearts and minds through Christ Jesus.* (The continuing presence of His peace in believers' lives.)

Prayer

Prince of Peace, I welcome Your peace into my heart and life today. Calm my fears, quiet my soul, and help me trust You fully. May Your peace flow through me to others this season. Amen.

Reflection Question

Where do you most need Christ's peace to reign in your life this Christmas?

Christmas calls us to surrender our worries and rest in the gentle reign of Christ's peace.

EIGHT

Out of Bethlehem

Micah 5:2 *But thou, Bethlehem Ephratah, though thou be little among the thousands of Judah, yet out of thee shall he come forth unto me that is to be ruler in Israel; whose goings forth have been from of old, from everlasting.*

Devotional Reading

Bethlehem was a small, seemingly insignificant town, yet God chose it as the birthplace of the Messiah. Micah prophesied centuries before Christ's birth that from this humble place would come a Ruler whose origins were eternal.

This reminds us that God delights in using what seems small to accomplish great things. The King of kings did not arrive in Rome or Jerusalem but in a manger in Bethlehem. God's ways are not our ways He chooses the weak things of the world to shame the strong (**1 Corinthians 1:27**).

Christmas invites us to see the beauty of humility. If God chose Bethlehem for His Son's arrival, He can also choose the hidden and overlooked places of our own lives to reveal His glory. No place, no person, is too small for His divine purpose.

God delights in using what seems small or forgotten to display His greatness. No place or season is too humble for His presence to shine through you.

Supportive Scriptures

1 Samuel 16:1 *And the Lord said unto Samuel, How long wilt thou mourn for Saul, seeing I have rejected him from reigning over Israel? fill thine horn with oil, and go, I will send thee to Jesse the Bethlehemite: for I have provided me a king among his sons.* **(The royal line of David and ultimately Christ begins in Bethlehem.)**

John 7:42 *Hath not the scripture said, That Christ cometh of the seed of David, and out of the town of Bethlehem, where David was?* **(Even the people of Jesus' day knew the Messiah must come from Bethlehem.)**

Prayer

Lord, thank You for choosing what the world overlooks to reveal Your glory. Help me to embrace humility, trusting that You can work powerfully through small places and small beginnings. Amen.

Reflection Question

What "small" or overlooked area in your life might God be preparing to use for His glory?

In God's hands, even the hidden places become holy ground

NINE

The Servant of the Lord

Isaiah 42:1 *Behold my servant, whom I uphold; mine elect, in whom my soul delighted; I have put my spirit upon him: he shall bring forth judgment to the Gentiles.*

Dwelling in the Word

Isaiah describes the Messiah as the Servant of the Lord chosen, Spirit-filled, and bringing justice to the nations. Unlike earthly rulers who dominate, Christ's kingship is marked by humility and service.

Jesus came not to be served but to serve and give His life as a ransom for many (**Mark 10:45** *For even the Son of man came not to be ministered unto, but to minister, and to give his life a ransom for many.*). The Servant would not shout or crush the weak; instead, He would tenderly care for the broken and lead with compassion. This prophecy points us to the gentle yet powerful ministry of Christ.

At Christmas, we celebrate not only the majesty of a King but the humility of a Servant. The One who was worshiped by angels stooped to wash feet. The One who created the world laid aside His glory to dwell among us. True greatness in God's kingdom is found in service.

Here are a few **meaningful ways to serve others this Christmas** that reflect the heart of Christ, who came not to be served but to serve:

Give Your Time

Visit someone who may be lonely, a neighbor, a nursing home resident, or a friend who's grieving. Your presence can be a gift of comfort and love.

Share a Meal

Prepare or deliver food to a family in need, a single parent, or someone spending the holidays alone. Just as Jesus fed others, we can share His compassion through simple acts of care.

Speak Life

Offer words of encouragement or write notes that remind others of their worth in Christ. A heartfelt message can lift weary hearts during this season.

Give Quietly

Bless someone anonymously pay for a meal, leave a grocery card, or meet a need without expecting recognition. Hidden generosity reflects the humility of Jesus' coming.

Pray for Others

Lift up those who are hurting, struggling, or searching for hope. Prayer is one of the most powerful ways to serve with Christlike love.

Forgive and Reconcile

Extend grace to someone you've been distant from. Christ came to bring peace, let His forgiveness flow through you to others.

Supportive Scriptures

Isaiah 61:1-2 *The Spirit of the Lord God is upon me; because the Lord hath anointed me to preach good tidings unto the meek; he hath sent me to bind up the brokenhearted, to proclaim liberty to the captives, and the opening of the prison to them that are bound.*

To proclaim the acceptable year of the Lord, and the day of vengeance of our God; to comfort all that mourn; **(The mission of the Servant proclaimed by Jesus Himself in Luke 4.)**

Acts 10:38 *How God anointed Jesus of Nazareth with the Holy Ghost and with power: who went about doing good and healing all that were oppressed of the devil; for God was with him.* **(Fulfills the image of the Spirit-filled Servant bringing justice and healing.)**

Prayer

Lord Jesus, thank You for being the Servant who came in humility to save us. Teach me to follow Your example of love, compassion, and selfless service. May I reflect Your servant-heart to those around me. Amen.

Reflection Question

In what ways can you serve others this Christmas season as a reflection of Christ's servant-heart?

TEN

Desire of All Nations

Haggai 2:7 *And I will shake all nations, and the desire of all nations shall come: and I will fill this house with glory, saith the LORD of hosts.*

Dwelling in the Word

Through the prophet Haggai, God promised that the "Desire of all nations" would come and fill His house with glory. This phrase points to Christ, the One who alone satisfies the deepest longings of every heart.

Every culture, every nation, and every generation shares a common ache for peace, hope, and redemption. While people search for fulfillment in wealth, power, or pleasure, the true Desire of all nations is found in Jesus. His birth was not for one people only, but for the whole world.

At Christmas, we are reminded that the glory of God is revealed not in a temple made with hands but in the person of Christ. He is the One who fills the emptiness of nations and the emptiness within our own hearts.

This Christmas, let your heart be a dwelling place for His presence. The same glory that filled the manger now desires to fill your life with light, hope, and unshakable peace.

Supporting Scriptures

Haggai 2:9 *The glory of this latter house shall be greater than of the former, saith the Lord of hosts: and in this place will I give peace, saith the Lord of hosts.* (Confirms that the glory and peace would come through the Messiah's presence.)

John 1:14 *And the Word was made flesh, and dwelt among us, (and we beheld his glory, the glory as of the only begotten of the Father,) full of grace and truth.* (The true glory fills the new "temple" Jesus Himself.)

Prayer

Father, thank You that Jesus is the Desire of all nations and the fulfillment of every longing heart. This Christmas, help me to look to Him alone for satisfaction and hope. Fill me with Your glory and presence. Amen.

Reflection Question

What desires in your heart are you tempted to fill with lesser things instead of Christ, the true Desire of all nations?

The Arrival of the Messiah

At last, the silence was broken. The promise that echoed through centuries took form in a humble manger beneath a Bethlehem sky. The Savior long awaited the Light of the world had come. Heaven's joy touched earth as angels proclaimed peace, and shepherds beheld the glory of God wrapped in swaddling clothes.

In these devotions, we pause to marvel at the wonder of Christ's birth the fulfillment of prophecy, the beauty of divine humility, and the love that came down to dwell among us. Each day invites you to draw nearer to the miracle of Emmanuel, to see beyond the simplicity of the stable and behold the majesty of the King who came to save.

ELEVEN

Emmanuel, God With Us

Matthew 1:23 *Behold, a virgin shall be with child, and shall bring forth a son, and they shall call his name Emmanuel, which being interpreted is, God with us.*

Dwelling in the Word

The angel's words to Joseph echo Isaiah's prophecy: the child born of Mary would be called Emmanuel, meaning *God with us*. This truth is the heart of Christmas. In Christ, God stepped into time, clothed Himself in flesh, and walked among His people.

Other religions point to men trying to reach up to God. Christmas tells the opposite story: God reaching down to us. He did not remain distant or detached. He came close, entering our world in humility so that we could know Him personally.

Emmanuel is not just a title it is a reality. God is not far from you. He is with you in joy and sorrow, in light and darkness, in victory and in struggle. The manger is proof of His nearness, and the cross is proof of His love.

Here are three powerful reminders to strengthen your faith and encourage your heart from this truth:

God's Presence Is Personal

Emmanuel means *God with us* not just in theory but in every moment. He walks beside you in ordinary days and difficult nights, reminding you that you are never alone.

God's Nearness Brings Comfort

Because Christ came close, you can find peace even in pain. His presence doesn't always remove the storm, but it steadies your heart within it.

God's Love Is Proven

The manger shows His willingness to come near; the cross shows how far His love will go. Both declare that you are seen, known, and deeply loved by Him.

Supporting Scriptures

Isaiah 7:14 *Behold, a virgin shall conceive, and bear a son, and shall call his name Immanuel.* (**The original prophecy fulfilled through Jesus' birth.**)

Colossians 2:9 *For in him dwelleth all the fulness of the Godhead bodily.* (**Confirms the divine nature of Jesus as God incarnate.**)

Prayer

Lord, thank You for being Emmanuel God with me. Help me to remember that I am never alone, for You are present in every moment. Teach me to walk in the assurance of Your nearness this season. Amen.

Reflection Question

Where do you most need to remember that God is *with you* right now?

When Jesus reigns in your heart, peace becomes your crown and love your way of life.

TWELVE

The Word Made Flesh

John 1:14 *And the Word was made flesh, and dwelt among us, (and we beheld his glory, the glory as of the only begotten of the Father,) full of grace and truth.*

Dwelling in the Word

John begins his Gospel not with shepherds or angels, but with eternity. The eternal Word, who was with God and was God, became flesh. He did not just appear like a man He truly took on our humanity and lived among us.

This is the mystery of the Incarnation: the Creator entered creation. The One who created the galaxies chose to speak in the language of humanity. The One who formed humanity from dust became dust Himself. He was full of grace bringing undeserved favor and full of truth revealing God's reality.

When we look at Jesus, we see the fullness of God revealed in human form. At Christmas, we are invited to behold His glory not distant but dwelling among us. The Word became flesh so that we could know God personally and intimately.

Here are **three ways we can grow to know God more intimately** through the truth that *the Word became flesh*:

Spend Time in His Word

Jesus is the living Word, and Scripture reveals His heart. As you read and meditate on His Word daily, you begin to recognize His voice and understand His character more deeply.

Cultivate Prayerful Conversation

Intimacy grows through honest, ongoing communication. Talk to God about everything your joys, your fears, your questions. As you listen in stillness, you'll sense His presence guiding and comforting you.

Walk in Obedience and Fellowship

The more we obey what we already know, the more He reveals Himself to us. Obedience opens the door to deeper fellowship, where His presence becomes not just known but experienced.

Supporting Scriptures

John 1:1–3 *In the beginning was the Word, and the Word was with God, and the Word was God. The same was in the beginning with God. All things were made by him; and without him was not anything made that was made.* **(Affirms that the Word Jesus is eternal and divine.)**

Colossians 1:15-17 *Who is the image of the invisible God, the firstborn of every creature: For by him were all things created, that are in heaven, and that are in earth, visible and invisible, whether they be thrones, or dominions, or principalities, or powers: all things were created by him, and for him: And he is before all things, and by him all things consist.* **(The Word made visible the Creator entering His creation.)**

Prayer

Lord Jesus, thank You for becoming flesh and dwelling among us. Thank You for revealing God's glory in a way we could see and understand. Help me to behold You this Christmas with fresh wonder and awe. Amen.

Reflection Question

How does the truth that "the Word became flesh" change the way you approach God in prayer and worship?

THIRTEEN

The Light of the World

John 8:12 *Then Spake Jesus again unto them, saying, I am the light of the world: he that follows me shall not walk in darkness, but shall have the light of life.*

Dwelling in the Word

In a world darkened by sin, Jesus declared Himself the Light of the world. Light exposes, guides, and brings life. Without light, we stumble; with light, we see clearly. The coming of Christ is the dawning of hope in the deepest night.

The first Christmas night was illuminated by the glory of God as angels filled the sky. But the true light was not in the heavens, it was lying in a manger. Jesus came to shine into our darkness, revealing truth and offering life.

The promise is not only cosmic but personal: "He that follows me shall not walk in darkness." When we choose to follow Him, His light directs our steps and chases away fear. The Christmas lights we hang in our homes are but small reminders of the greater Light who has come.

Supporting Scriptures

John 1:4–5 *In him was life; and the life was the light of men. And the light shineth in darkness; and the darkness comprehended it*

not.
(Jesus, the eternal Word, brings divine light that no darkness can overcome.)

John 1:9 *That was the true Light, which lights every man that comes into the world.*
(Christ is the universal and true Light for all humanity.)

Prayer

Light of the world, shine into my heart and scatter every shadow of fear, sin, and doubt. Guide my steps and help me walk in the light of Your truth. Let Your light shine through me this Christmas. Amen.

Reflection Question

What areas of your life feel dark right now, and how can you invite Christ's light to shine there?

The lights we hang at Christmas shine to remind us of the true Light who brightens every heart, Jesus Christ.

FOURTEEN

The Good Shepherd

John 10:11 *I am the good shepherd: the good shepherd giveth his life for the sheep.*

Dwelling in the Word

Shepherds were the first to hear the angelic announcement of Christ's birth. How fitting, then, that Jesus would later describe Himself as the Good Shepherd. Unlike hired hands who abandon the flock when danger comes, the Good Shepherd lays down His life for the sheep.

This picture reminds us of both His tenderness and His sacrifice. Shepherds guide, protect, and provide. Jesus does all this perfectly. He knows His sheep by name, and His sheep know His voice. Christmas reminds us that the baby in the manger is not distant He is the Shepherd who draws near, who cares for us, and who ultimately gave His life for our salvation.

In a noisy, chaotic world, it is easy to follow the wrong voices. But the Good Shepherd still calls today, leading His people to green pastures and still waters. If we listen and follow, we will find rest for our souls.

Here are four meaningful ways we can walk closely with Christ in the midst of today's world:

Quiet the Noise

Set aside moments each day to step away from distractions social media, busyness, and worry. Create space to hear the still, gentle voice of the Shepherd through prayer and Scripture.

Stay Rooted in God's Word

The voice of the Good Shepherd is clear in His Word. Let the Bible be your daily guide so you can discern truth from the noise and follow His direction with confidence.

Walk in Obedience and Trust

Following Christ means trusting His lead even when the path is uncertain. Obedience invites peace; trust opens the way to green pastures of rest.

Stay Close to His Flock

Surround yourself with other believers who encourage and sharpen your faith. In community, we stay connected to the Shepherd and find strength to keep following Him faithfully.

Supportive Scriptures

Psalm 23:1-3 *The Lord is my shepherd; I shall not want. He maketh me to lie down in green pastures: he leadeth me beside the still waters. He restoreth my soul: he leadeth me in the paths of righteousness for his name's sake.* **(The foundational picture of God as Shepherd fulfilled perfectly in Jesus.)**

Isaiah 40:11 *He shall feed his flock like a shepherd: he shall gather the lambs with his arm, and carry them in his bosom, and shall gently lead those that are with young.* **(A prophecy showing the Messiah's tender care for His people.)**

Prayer

Jesus, my Good Shepherd, thank You for knowing me by name and caring for me so deeply. Help me to hear Your voice above all others and to trust You to lead me. Thank You for laying down Your life for me. Amen.

Reflection Question

How can you tune your heart more closely to the Shepherd's voice this Christmas season?

FIFTEEN

The Lamb of God

John 1:29 *The next day John saw Jesus coming unto him, and said, Behold the Lamb of God, which taketh away the sin of the world.*

Dwelling in the Word

When John the Baptist first saw Jesus, he identified Him not as a teacher, prophet, or miracle-worker but as the Lamb of God. This title carries the weight of centuries of sacrifice, from the lamb at Passover to the daily temple offerings. Every lamb that had ever been slain pointed to this moment.

Jesus came to be our substitute, to bear the penalty of sin, and to remove its power forever. The cradle in Bethlehem pointed to the cross at Calvary. Christmas and Easter are inseparably linked, for the purpose of His coming was to take away the sins of the world.

At Christmas, it's easy to focus on the innocence of a newborn child. Yet we must also remember the mission: the Lamb was born to die. And through His sacrifice, we find forgiveness, freedom, and eternal life.

Here are three meaningful truths to reflect on as we remember the deeper purpose of Christ's coming:

The Manger Points to the Cross

Jesus' birth was not the end of the story it was the beginning of God's plan of redemption. The cradle leads to the cross, where love was fully revealed.

His Sacrifice Brings Our Freedom

Christ came to break the power of sin and open the way to forgiveness. What began in Bethlehem was fulfilled at Calvary so we could live free and restored.

His Death Gives Us Eternal Hope

Because the Lamb was willing to die, we now have the promise of eternal life. Christmas reminds us not just of His coming, but of the life and victory He secured for us.

Supporting Scriptures

Isaiah 53:7 *He is brought as a lamb to the slaughter, and as a sheep before her shearers is dumb, so he open not his mouth.*
(Prophecy of the suffering Messiah's silent submission.)

1 Corinthians 5:7 For even Christ our Passover is sacrificed for us.
(Paul directly connects Jesus to the Passover lamb.)

Prayer

Thank You, Lord Jesus, for being the Lamb of God who takes away the sin of the world. Thank You that my sins are forgiven because of Your sacrifice. Help me to live in the freedom and gratitude of that truth this Christmas. Amen.

Reflection Question

What does it mean to you personally that Jesus came as the Lamb of God to take away your sin?

Behold the Lamb of God gentle in humility, mighty in salvation.

SIXTEEN

The Son of David

Luke 1:32 *He shall be great, and shall be called the Son of the Highest: and the Lord God shall give unto him the throne of his father David.*

Dwelling in the Word

When the angel spoke to Mary, he declared that her child would be given "the throne of His father David." This connected Jesus directly to God's covenant promise that David's throne would endure forever (**2 Samuel 7:16** *And thine house and thy kingdom shall be established for ever before thee: thy throne shall be established forever.*)

Jesus is the fulfillment of this promise the true and eternal King from David's line. Though He entered the world in humility, His reign is everlasting. He is not just the Son of Mary but the Son of David, the rightful heir whose kingdom will never end.

Christmas reminds us that God keeps covenant promises, no matter how long the wait. From David to Mary spanned nearly a thousand years, yet the promise was fulfilled exactly as God said. In a world where promises are easily broken, the faithfulness of God shines brightly in the story of Christ.

Christmas reminds us to fix our hearts and minds on the One who never fails. God's faithfulness endures through every delay and every season of waiting. As we reflect on Christ, may we rest in the assurance that what He promises, He will always bring to pass.

Supportive Scriptures

2 Samuel 7:12-13 *And when thy days be fulfilled, and thou shalt sleep with thy fathers, I will set up thy seed after thee, which shall proceed out of thy bowels, and I will establish his kingdom. He shall build an house for my name, and I will stablish the throne of his kingdom forever.* (The original covenant promise God made to David fulfilled in Christ.)

Psalm 89:3-4 *I have made a covenant with my chosen, I have sworn unto David my servant, Thy seed will I establish forever and build up thy throne to all generations. Selah.* (God's unbreakable promise of an eternal dynasty through David's line.)

Prayer

Faithful God, thank You for keeping Your promises throughout history and in my own life. Thank You that Jesus is the Son of David and the eternal King. Help me to trust Your Word and live under the authority of Christ's reign. Amen.

Reflection Question

How does the fulfillment of God's promise to David encourage you to trust Him with the promises He has spoken over your life?

Jesus, the Son of the Highest, reigns with everlasting greatness and unshakable authority.

SEVENTEEN

The Son of God

Luke 1:35 *And the angel answered and said unto her, The Holy Ghost shall come upon thee, and the power of the Highest shall overshadow thee: therefore also that holy thing which shall be born of thee shall be called the Son of God.*

Dwelling in the Word

When the angel explained the miraculous conception to Mary, he gave Jesus the title *Son of God*. This was no ordinary child He was fully divine, conceived by the power of the Holy Spirit. His birth was unlike any in history, for He entered the world both human and divine.

The title *Son of God* affirms Jesus' unique relationship with the Father. He is not just a teacher or prophet but the very expression of God's nature (**Hebrews 1:3** *Who being the brightness of his glory, and the express image of his person, and upholding all things by the word of his power, when he had by himself purged our sins, sat down on the right hand of the Majesty on high:*). The cradle in Bethlehem held the One through whom all things were made.

Christmas calls us to marvel at this mystery: the eternal Son humbled Himself to take on flesh. This truth not only assures us of His authority but also of His ability to save. Only the Son of God could break sin's curse and bring us back into fellowship with the Father.

Supporting Scriptures

Isaiah 7:14 *Therefore the Lord himself shall give you a sign; Behold, a virgin shall conceive, and bear a son, and shall call his name Immanuel.* **(Prophecy fulfilled through the virgin birth "God with us.")**

Luke 3:22 *And the Holy Ghost descended in a bodily shape like a dove upon him, and a voice came from heaven, which said, Thou art my beloved Son; in thee I am well pleased.* **(Reaffirms His divine sonship through the Spirit's witness.)**

Prayer

Son of God, I stand in awe of the mystery of Your coming. Thank You for humbling Yourself to be born as one of us so that we could know salvation. Teach me to worship You with reverence and gratitude this season. Amen.

Reflection Question

How does the truth that Jesus is the Son of God strengthen your faith in His power to save?

The power of the Highest still works wonders what He births by His Spirit will reveal His glory.

EIGHTEEN

The Bread of Life

John 6:35 *And Jesus said unto them, I am the bread of life: he that cometh to me shall never hunger; and he that believeth on me shall never thirst.*

Dwelling in the Word

Food sustains life, yet it can only satisfy for a short time. Jesus declared Himself the Bread of Life, offering nourishment that satisfies eternally. Just as bread was the staple of daily life in biblical times, Christ is the essential source of spiritual life for all who believe.

Christmas reminds us that God not only provided physical bread, like manna in the wilderness (**Exodus 16:14**), but the true bread from heaven His Son. The child in the manger would grow to say, "Whoever comes to me will never hunger."

In a season filled with abundance tables full of food, homes full of gifts it is easy to overlook the One who truly satisfies. But no amount of holiday feasting can fill the emptiness of the soul. Only Christ, the Bread of Life, can.

Here are three ways we can allow Christ to fill our empty souls this Christmas season:

Make Room for His Presence

Slow down and create quiet moments amid the noise and celebration. Invite Jesus into your heart daily through prayer and reflection He fills what hurry and distraction cannot.

Feast on His Word

Just as we nourish our bodies with food, our souls are fed by Scripture. Spend time reading the Word and let His truth satisfy the deepest hunger within you.

Share His Love with Others

When we pour out love, kindness, and generosity, Christ's life flows through us. Giving of ourselves is one of the sweetest ways to experience the fullness of His presence.

Supportive Scriptures

John 6:33 *For the bread of God is he which comes down from heaven and gives life unto the world.*
(Christ gives divine, life-giving nourishment to all who believe.)

Matthew 5:6 *Blessed are they which do hunger and thirst after righteousness: for they shall be filled.*
(Spiritual hunger is satisfied in the righteousness of Christ.)

Prayer

Lord Jesus, You are the Bread of Life. I come to You hungry and thirsty, and I thank You for satisfying the deepest longings of my soul. Help me to feed daily on Your Word and presence this season. Amen.

Reflection Question

What "hungers" or longings in your life are you tempted to fill with temporary things instead of Christ, the Bread of Life?

NINETEEN

The Way, the Truth, and the Life

John 14:6 *Jesus saith unto him, I am the way, the truth, and the life: no man cometh unto the Father, but by me.*

Dwelling in the Word

In a world of many paths, competing voices, and fleeting promises, Jesus declared Himself the only Way to the Father, the ultimate Truth, and the very source of Life. This is an exclusive claim, yet it is also the most inclusive invitation: all are welcome, but only through Him.

Christmas shows us that God made the way to Himself not by human effort but by sending His Son. The manger points to the cross, where the Way was opened, the Truth revealed, and Life made available to all.

The holiday season often tempts us with distractions many "ways" to happiness, many "truths" to follow, many "lives" to pursue. But Jesus reminds us that only in Him are these found. He is not one option among many; He is the only answer.

Here are three truths to hold close as we journey through this Christmas season:

The Way

In a season filled with many paths to fulfillment, Jesus is the only road that truly leads home to the Father.

The Truth

When the world offers countless versions of truth, Jesus remains the unchanging Word that reveals what is real and lasting.

The Life

Amid temporary joys and fading pleasures, Jesus is the life that fills the heart with eternal purpose and peace.

Supportive Scriptures

John 10:9 *I am the door: by me if any man enter in, he shall be saved.*(Christ is the entrance to salvation and relationship with the Father.)

John 17:17 *Sanctify them through thy truth: thy word is truth.* (Jesus' prayer reveals that God's truth purifies and transforms.)

1 John 5:11-12 *And this is the record, that God hath given to us eternal life, and this life is in his Son. He that hath the Son hath life; and he that hath not the Son of God hath not life.* (Life is not found in religion or works only in Jesus.)

Prayer

Lord Jesus, thank You for being the Way, the Truth, and the Life. Forgive me when I look for life in lesser things. Help me to follow Your way, believe Your truth, and live in the fullness of Your life this Christmas. Amen.

Reflection Question

What is one area where you need to stop relying on your own way and trust fully in Jesus as the Way, the Truth, and the Life?

TWENTY

The King of Kings

Revelation 19:16 *And he has on his vesture and on his thigh a name written, KING OF KINGS, AND LORD OF LORDS.*

Dwelling in the Word

The baby born in Bethlehem is not only Savior but King the King above all kings, the Lord above all lords. His first coming was in humility, wrapped in swaddling clothes, but His second coming will be in glory, clothed in majesty.

At Christmas, we celebrate His birth, but we also look forward to His return. The One who lay in a manger will one day reign openly over all creation. Every knee will bow, and every tongue will confess that He is Lord (**Philippians 2:10–11** *That at the name of Jesus every knee should bow, of things in heaven, and things in earth, and things under the earth; And that every tongue should confess that Jesus Christ is Lord, to the glory of God the Father*).

This truth gives us hope. The kingdoms of this world are fragile, but His kingdom is unshakable. The King of kings rules with justice and mercy, and He invites us to live under His reign now, awaiting the day when His rule will be complete.

Here are three reminders about Jesus' unshakable Kingdom that encourage us to stay grounded in the Word of God:

His Kingdom Is Built on Eternal Truth

While the world's systems shift and fail, God's Word stands forever. When we anchor our lives in Scripture, we build on a foundation that cannot be moved.

His Reign Brings Peace and Justice

Christ's rule is not marked by fear or corruption but by righteousness, mercy, and peace. Studying His Word helps us reflect His heart and live as citizens of His Kingdom even now.

His Kingdom Is Already at Work Within Us

Every time we choose faith over fear, love over division, and obedience over compromise, we reveal the power of His unshakable Kingdom. The Word of God keeps our hearts aligned with the King until His reign is fully revealed.

Supportive Scriptures

1 Timothy 6:14-15 *That thou keep this commandment without spot, unrebukable, until the appearing of our Lord Jesus Christ: Which in his times he shall shew, who is the blessed and only Potentate, the King of kings, and Lord of lords;* **(Paul declares Christ's absolute and unrivaled dominion.)**

Revelation 17:14 *These shall make war with the Lamb, and the Lamb shall overcome them: for he is Lord of lords, and King of kings.* **(Christ's title affirmed before His final victory.)**

Prayer

King Jesus, I bow before You as the King of kings and Lord of lords. Thank You that Your reign is eternal and unshakable.

This Christmas, help me to live with hope and confidence in Your coming kingdom. Amen.

Reflection Question

How does remembering that Christ is the King of kings affect the way you view the world's troubles today?

Jesus reigns supreme King of kings, Lord of lords, and the Victor whose rule will never end.

The Nativity and Christmas Fulfillment

The night that changed the world had come heaven's promise fulfilled in the cry of a newborn King. In the stillness of Bethlehem, prophecy met reality, and the Word became flesh to dwell among us. Every detail of the nativity the manger, the star, the humble worship of shepherds and wise men tells the story of God's faithfulness and love reaching its perfect completion in Christ.

In these final devotions, we reflect on the beauty and wonder of that holy night and what it means for us today. Christmas is not only a celebration of His birth but a revelation of His purpose to bring light to every heart and redemption to all who believe. As you read, may your soul rest in the truth that the long-awaited Savior has come, and in Him, every promise of God finds its "Yes" and "Amen."

TWENTY-ONE

Gabriel's Announcement to Mary

Luke 1:26-28 *And in the sixth month the angel Gabriel was sent from God unto a city of Galilee, named Nazareth, To a virgin espoused to a man whose name was Joseph, of the house of David; and the virgin's name was Mary. And the angel came in unto her, and said, Hail, thou that art highly favored, the Lord is with thee: blessed art thou among women.*

Dwelling in the Word

When Gabriel appeared to Mary, he announced the impossible: that she, a virgin, would bear the Son of God. This moment reminds us that God delights in choosing the unlikely and accomplishing the impossible. Mary was young, obscure, and from Nazareth a town of little reputation yet God set His favor upon her.

Christmas begins with God's grace finding us where we are. Just as Mary's life was forever changed by God's Word, so our lives are transformed when we receive His promises in faith. Her response, "Be it unto me according to thy word," is an example of humble surrender.

This season, may we, like Mary, respond with faith to God's calling, no matter how daunting or unexpected it may seem.

Here are three ways believers can respond by faith to God's calling, inspired by Mary's example:

Trust God's Word Above Your Feelings

Mary didn't understand everything the angel said, but she believed God's promise. Faith begins when we choose trust over fear and stand on what He has spoken.

Surrender Your Plans to His Purpose

Mary's "yes" changed the course of her life and history. When we yield our will to God's, He turns ordinary obedience into extraordinary impact.

Walk in Humble Confidence

Like Mary, we can move forward knowing that if God called us, He would equip us. Faith doesn't require knowing the outcome just trusting the One who leads the way.

Supportive Scriptures

Luke 1:19 *And the angel answering said unto him, I am Gabriel, that stand in the presence of God; and am sent to speak unto thee, and to shew thee these glad tidings.* (Confirms Gabriel's heavenly authority also appearing to Zacharias before Mary.)

Luke 1:30–31 *And the angel said unto her, Fear not, Mary: for thou hast found favor with God.*
And, behold, thou shalt conceive in thy womb, and bring forth a son, and shalt call his name JESUS.
(Continues the announcement highlighting divine favor and promise.)

Prayer

Lord, thank You for choosing the humble to display Your glory. Give me a heart like Mary's willing to trust and obey, even when I do not understand. May I live surrendered to Your Word. Amen.

Reflection Question

Where is God inviting you to trust His Word more deeply, even when it seems impossible?

TWENTY-TWO

Joseph's Dream

Matthew 1:20–21 *But while he thought on these things, behold, the angel of the Lord appeared unto him in a dream, saying, Joseph, thou son of David, fear not to take unto thee Mary thy wife: for that which is conceived in her is of the Holy Ghost. And she shall bring forth a son, and thou shalt call his name JESUS: for he shall save his people from their sins.*

Dwelling in the Word

Joseph faced confusion and fear when he learned of Mary's pregnancy. Yet God intervened through a dream, assuring him that this was His plan and instructing him to name the child *Jesus*, meaning "the Lord saves."

Christmas is not only about God's power but also about His reassurance. Just as Joseph was told not to fear, we too are invited to trust God's plans, even when they upend our expectations. Jesus' very name reminds us that His mission is to save His people from their sins.

Sometimes obedience to God requires courage. Joseph's faith preserved Mary's honor, protected the child, and played a vital role in God's story. Christmas calls us to the same obedience, trusting God when the path is hard.

Here are three ways trusting God in hard times helps believers, inspired by Joseph's obedience and faith:

Trust Leads to Courageous Obedience

Joseph obeyed even when it was difficult and uncertain. When we trust God, He gives us the courage to follow His will, even when others may not understand our choices.

Trust Aligns Us with God's Greater Purpose

Joseph's quiet faith positioned him within God's divine plan. In the same way, our obedience during hard seasons allows God to work through us to accomplish things far beyond what we can see.

Trust Brings Peace in the Midst of Fear

Though Joseph faced confusion and pressure, his trust in God brought peace to his heart. When we rest in God's direction, He replaces anxiety with assurance, reminding us that His plans are always good.

Supportive Scriptures

Genesis 37:5 *And Joseph dreamed a dream, and he told it his brethren...*
(Another Joseph who received divine revelation through dreams.)

Daniel 2:19 *Then was the secret revealed unto Daniel in a night vision. Then Daniel blessed the God of heaven.* (God gives understanding and direction through dreams and visions.)

Prayer

Lord, thank You for showing Joseph that Your ways are higher than ours. Teach me to trust You when I do not understand, and to walk in courageous obedience to Your Word. Amen.

Reflection Question

What step of obedience is God asking you to take this season, even if it feels costly?

TWENTY-THREE

Mary's Song

Luke 1:46–47 *And Mary said, My soul doth magnify the Lord, and my spirit hath rejoiced in God my Saviour.*

Dwelling in the Word

After receiving the angel's message and visiting Elizabeth, Mary burst into a song of praise, known as the *Magnificat*. Her words overflowed with gratitude and awe at God's mercy, faithfulness, and power.

Mary's song reminds us that worship is the natural response to God's work in our lives. She praised not only for what God had done for her personally but also for His faithfulness to Israel throughout generations.

This Christmas, we are invited to join in Mary's song. Our souls can magnify the Lord as we remember His faithfulness, rejoice in His salvation, and celebrate His mercy that extends to all who fear Him.

This Christmas, let your heart echo Mary's song full of gratitude, awe, and trust. When we pause to remember God's goodness, our worship becomes a testimony of His faithfulness through every generation. May your soul magnify the Lord, for He has done great things.

Supportive Scriptures

Psalm 100:5 *For the Lord is good; his mercy is everlasting; and his truth endures to all generations.*
(God's unchanging mercy echoed in Mary's praise.)

Psalm 98:3 He hath remembered his mercy and his truth toward the house of Israel.
(God's faithfulness across generations celebrated in song.)

Prayer

Lord, fill my heart with gratitude and worship this season. May my soul magnify You in every circumstance, and may my life be a song of praise to Your faithfulness. Amen.

Reflection Question

What reasons do you have to magnify the Lord with thanksgiving this Christmas?

When our hearts remember His goodness, praise becomes the song our souls can't help but sing.

TWENTY-FOUR

The Journey to Bethlehem

Luke 2:4–5 *And Joseph also went up from Galilee, out of the city of Nazareth, into Judaea, unto the city of David, which is called Bethlehem (because he was of the house and lineage of David) to be taxed with Mary his espoused wife, being great with child.*

Dwelling in the Word

The journey from Nazareth to Bethlehem was long and difficult, especially for Mary, heavily pregnant. Yet it was ordained by God, fulfilling the prophecy that the Messiah would be born in Bethlehem (**Micah 5:2**).

This reminds us that God uses even the decrees of earthly rulers and the challenges of life to accomplish His purposes. What looked like an inconvenient journey was part of a divine plan.

In our own lives, we often face unexpected detours and hardships. But Christmas reminds us that God is sovereign over every step. Even when the road is hard, He is guiding us toward His promises.

Here are three encouraging ways we can remain hopeful and trust God through life's difficult seasons:

Remember That Every Detour Has Purpose

Just as Joseph and Mary's journey to Bethlehem seemed difficult yet fulfilled prophecy, our setbacks can be setups for

God's greater plan. Trust that He's working even when the path feels inconvenient.

Focus on God's Presence, Not the Problem

In every hardship, God walks beside us. When we shift our focus from what's going wrong to who is with us, peace replaces frustration, and faith begins to grow.

Hold On to His Promises

The road may be rough, but it leads to fulfillment. Keep your eyes on God's promises, knowing His timing is perfect and His plans are always for your good.

Supportive Scriptures

2 Samuel 7:12-13 *And when thy days be fulfilled, and thou shalt sleep with thy fathers, I will set up thy seed after thee, which shall proceed out of thy bowels, and I will establish his kingdom. He shall build an house for my name, and I will stablish the throne of his kingdom forever.* **(Confirms that the Messiah would come from David's line, which explains Joseph's connection to Bethlehem the City of David.)**

Micah 5:2 *But thou, Bethlehem Ephratah, though thou be little among the thousands of Judah, yet out of thee shall he come forth unto me that is to be ruler in Israel; whose goings forth have been from of old, from everlasting.* **(Foretells that the Messiah would be born in Bethlehem perfectly fulfilled through this journey.)**

Prayer

Lord, help me to trust that every step of my journey is in Your hands. When the road is difficult, remind me that You are working all things for Your glory and my good. Amen.

Reflection Question

How can you trust God more fully in the "detours" and difficulties of your journey?

TWENTY-FIVE

The Savior Is Born

Luke 2:6–7 *And so it was, that, while they were there, the days were accomplished that she should be delivered. And she brought forth her firstborn son, and wrapped him in swaddling clothes, and laid him in a manger; because there was no room for them in the inn.*

Dwelling in the Word

The moment all of history had awaited arrived quietly in Bethlehem. The Savior of the world entered not a palace but a manger, wrapped in simple cloth, born to humble parents. Heaven's glory was clothed in humanity's frailty.

The simplicity of Christ's birth is a reminder that God's glory often comes in unexpected ways. The King of kings came not in majesty but in meekness, identifying with the lowly and the poor.

At Christmas, we celebrate not only the fact of His birth but the wonder of His humility. The Son of God made room for us by entering our world. The question is: will we make room for Him in our hearts?

Here are a few meaningful ways we can make room for God in our hearts this Christmas:

Slow Down and Create Space for His Presence

In the midst of the holiday rush, take intentional moments of stillness to pray, reflect, and listen. God often speaks in the quiet places of a surrendered heart.

Welcome Him Through His Word

Spend time reading Scripture each day. As you meditate on His truth, your heart becomes a dwelling place for His wisdom, peace, and joy.

Let Go of Distractions and Worry

Making room for God often means clearing out what competes for our attention. Release fear, busyness, or anything that crowds out His presence.

Serve Others with Love

Every act of kindness and humility mirrors the heart of Christ. When we love others selflessly, we make room for Him to live and move through us.

Supportive Scriptures

Isaiah 7:14 *Therefore the Lord himself shall give you a sign; Behold, a virgin shall conceive, and bear a son, and shall call his name Immanuel.* **(Foretold the virgin birth God dwelling among His people.)**

Isaiah 9:6-7 *For unto us a child is born, unto us a son is given: and the government shall be upon his shoulder: and his name shall be called Wonderful, Counsellor, The mighty God, The everlasting Father, The Prince of Peace. Of the increase of his government and peace there shall be no end, upon the throne of David, and upon his kingdom, to order it, and to establish it with judgment and with justice from henceforth even forever. The zeal of the Lord of hosts will perform this.* **(Reveals the divine identity and eternal reign of the newborn Child.)**

Prayer

Lord Jesus, thank You for humbling Yourself to be born as a child. Thank You for entering our world to bring salvation. Help me to make room for You in my heart this Christmas. Amen.

Reflection Question

What distractions or "crowded rooms" in your life need to be cleared to make room for Christ this season?

TWENTY-SIX

The Angels' Song

Luke 2:13–14 *And suddenly there was with the angel a multitude of the heavenly host praising God, and saying, Glory to God in the highest, and on earth peace, good will toward men.*

Dwelling in the Word

The night sky over Bethlehem exploded with light and song as angels proclaimed the birth of the Savior. Their message was clear: glory belongs to God, and peace is now available to humankind through Christ.

Heaven rejoiced at His coming. The angels' song reminds us that Christmas is ultimately about worship lifting glory to God for His gift of salvation. It also reminds us that true peace comes not through politics or possessions but through the presence of Christ.

As we hear Christmas carols and songs this season, may we join the angels in declaring glory to God and peace on earth. Worship is the right response to the gift of Jesus.

Here are a few ways believers can be reminded to declare Glory to God and peace on earth as we hear carols this Christmas season:

Turn Listening into Worship

When you hear Christmas carols, pause and let the lyrics lead you into praise. Don't just listen worship. Let every note remind you of the Savior's greatness and grace.

Speak Words of Peace and Gratitude

Just as the angels declared peace on earth, we can echo that message through our words offering encouragement, forgiveness, and kindness to others.

Reflect on the Meaning Behind the Music

Take time to meditate on the truths each song proclaims God's glory revealed in Christ, His mercy extended to all. Let those truths renew your joy and deepen your faith.

Share the Message of Peace

Use the songs of the season as opportunities to share hope. Whether through a simple conversation or a heartfelt post, declare that true peace is found in Jesus Christ alone.

Supportive Scriptures

Psalm 148:1–2 *Praise ye the Lord. Praise ye the Lord from the heavens: praise him in the heights. Praise ye him, all his angels. Praise ye him, all his hosts.*
(Heaven and its hosts were created to glorify God now fulfilled in praise at the birth of His Son.)

Isaiah 6:3 *And one cried unto another, and said, Holy, holy, holy, is the Lord of hosts: the whole earth is full of his glory.*
(Echoes the angelic chorus heaven and earth united in glory to God.)

Prayer

Glorious God, I join the angels in giving You praise. Thank You for bringing peace through Jesus Christ. May my life this Christmas be a song of worship to Your name. Amen.

Reflection Question

How can you intentionally give glory to God in your words and actions this season?

TWENTY-SEVEN

The Shepherds Worship

Luke 2:15–16 *And it came to pass, as the angels were gone away from them into heaven, the shepherds said one to another, Let us now go even unto Bethlehem, and see this thing which is come to pass, which the Lord hath made known unto us. And they came with haste, and found Mary, and Joseph, and the babe lying in a manger.*

Dwelling in the Word

The shepherds, after hearing the angels' message, wasted no time. They went "with haste" to see the newborn King. Their response models how we too should respond to the good news with urgency, faith, and worship.

Shepherds were ordinary people, often overlooked in society, yet they were the first invited to witness the miracle of Christ's birth. This shows us that the gospel is for everyone rich and poor, known and unknown.

Like the shepherds, we are called not just to hear the good news but to seek Christ personally and worship Him with joy.

And just as the shepherds shared what they had seen and heard, we too are called to tell others about the Savior. The wonder of Christmas is not meant to be kept to ourselves, it's a message meant to shine through our words, actions, and lives. When we share the good news, we continue the song of heaven: *"Glory to God in the highest, and on earth peace, goodwill toward men."*

Here are a few meaningful points that remind us how to let the wonder of Christmas shine through our lives:

Share the Message of Hope

Tell others about what Christ has done in your life. A simple testimony or word of encouragement can point someone to the true meaning of Christmas.

Reflect Christ's Love in Your Actions

Show kindness, forgiveness, and compassion in everyday moments. Small acts of love often speak louder than words.

Live with Joy and Gratitude

Let the joy of knowing Christ be evident in your attitude. A thankful heart becomes a living invitation for others to experience His goodness.

Be a Light in a Dark World

In a season that can feel rushed or heavy for many, your peace and faith can shine as a quiet testimony of God's presence.

Keep Christ at the Center

Remember that Christmas isn't just a date it's a declaration that God is with us. Let every celebration, conversation, and decision reflect His glory.

Supportive Scriptures

James 4:6 *God resisted the proud, but giveth grace unto the humble.* **(The shepherds' simple hearts made them ready to receive God's grace.)**

Hebrews 11:6 *He that cometh to God must believe that he is, and that he is a rewarder of them that diligently seek him.* (The shepherds' journey to Bethlehem reflects faith in action.)

Prayer

Lord, thank You for inviting the shepherds to witness the birth of Christ. Thank You that the gospel is for all people, including me. Help me to seek You with eagerness and worship You with joy. Amen.

Reflection Question

What would it look like for you to "go with haste" to pursue Christ more fully this Christmas?

TWENTY-EIGHT

Simeon & Anna Awaited Him

Luke 2:30–32 *For mine eyes have seen thy salvation, which thou hast prepared before the face of all people; a light to lighten the Gentiles, and the glory of thy people Israel.*

Dwelling in the Word

In the temple, Simeon and Anna, both devout and waiting on God's promises, recognized Jesus as the Messiah. Simeon declared that he had seen God's salvation a light for the Gentiles and glory for Israel.

Their faith reminds us that waiting on God is never wasted. For years, they held to God's promise, and at just the right time, their hope was fulfilled in Christ.

Christmas is not only about the moment of Christ's birth but also about God's perfect timing. Just as Simeon and Anna waited expectantly, we too wait for Christ's return. Their story encourages us to remain faithful, trusting that God always keeps His Word.

Here are three reminders to strengthen your faith and encourage you to trust that God always fulfills His Word:

God's Timing Is Always Perfect

Simeon and Anna waited patiently, and at just the right moment, they saw God's promise fulfilled. Delays are not denials what God has spoken will come to pass in His perfect time.

Faithfulness in Waiting Bears Fruit

While they waited, Simeon and Anna stayed devoted in prayer and worship. Likewise, our waiting seasons are opportunities to grow in faith, deepen our trust, and strengthen our relationship with God.

God Always Fulfills His Promises

Every prophecy about Christ's coming was fulfilled, proving that God's Word never fails. As we wait for Christ's return, we can live with confidence that His promises remain sure and steadfast.

Supportive Scriptures

Isaiah 49:6 *I will also give thee for a light to the Gentiles, that thou mayest be my salvation unto the end of the earth.* (**A perfect reflection of Simeon's prophetic praise in the temple.**)

Isaiah 52:10 *The Lord hath made bare his holy arm in the eyes of all the nations; and all the ends of the earth shall see the salvation of our God.* (**A vision of God's salvation revealed openly fulfilled in Christ's birth.**)

Prayer

Lord, teach me to wait with faith like Simeon and Anna. Help me to trust Your timing and hold fast to Your promises. Thank You that in Jesus I see Your salvation. Amen.

Reflection Question

How can Simeon and Anna's example of patient faith encourage you in what you are waiting for today?

TWENTY-NINE

The Visit of the Wise Men

Matthew 2:10–11 *When they saw the star, they rejoiced with exceeding great joy. And when they were come into the house, they saw the young child with Mary, his mother, and fell down, and worshipped him: and when they had opened their treasures, they presented unto him gifts; gold, and frankincense, and myrrh.*

Dwelling in the Word

The wise men traveled from afar, guided by a star, seeking the newborn King. When they found Him, they fell in worship and offered gifts gold for His kingship, frankincense for His deity, and myrrh for His suffering.

Their journey reminds us that true wisdom is found in seeking Christ above all else. They left behind comfort, traveled great distance, and gave costly gifts all to honor Jesus.

This Christmas, we are called to the same joyful worship, sacrificial giving, and wholehearted devotion. Christ is worthy of nothing less.

Here are a few heartfelt reminders to guide our response to Christ's gift this Christmas:

Worship with Joyful Hearts

Like the wise men who rejoiced at finding the Savior, let our worship be filled with gratitude and awe. True joy is found in honoring Christ above all else.

Give with a Willing Spirit

The wise men offered their best gifts to Jesus. We too can give generously our time, talents, and love to reflect His heart of giving.

Devote Yourself Fully to Christ

Christmas reminds us that Jesus deserves our whole hearts, not just a portion of our attention. Let every area of your life your words, actions, and choices declare that He is worthy.

Live Out Your Worship Daily

Worship doesn't end when the carols stop. Let your daily obedience, kindness, and faith be a continual offering of love to the One who gave everything for you.

Supportive Scriptures

Psalm 72:10–11 *The kings of Tarshish and of the isles shall bring presents: the kings of Sheba and Seba shall offer gifts. Yea, all kings shall fall down before him: all nations shall serve him.* (A messianic prophecy prefiguring the wise men's offering of gifts and worship.)

Matthew 2:2 *Where is he that is born King of the Jews? for we have seen his star in the east and are come to worship him.* (The wise men confirm their journey was guided by divine revelation.)

Prayer

Lord, like the wise men, may I seek You with diligence, worship You with reverence, and offer You my very best. You are worthy of all honor and praise. Amen.

Reflection Question

What "gifts" can you offer Christ this season your time, your worship, your obedience, your resources?

THIRTY

The Word Dwelling Among Us

John 1:14 *And the Word was made flesh, and dwelt among us, (and we beheld his glory, the glory as of the only begotten of the Father,) full of grace and truth.*

Dwelling in the Word

We end where John begins with the Word made flesh. The Christmas story is not just about a baby's birth but about God dwelling among His people. Christ came to live with us so that we could live with Him forever.

The glory seen in the manger was the glory of God Himself, full of grace and truth. Christmas is not the end of the story but the beginning of a new covenant, a new hope, and a new life in Christ.

As we close this 30-day journey, may we remember that Christmas is not just a season but a Savior. The Word who dwelt among us still dwells within us by His Spirit. And one day, we will dwell with Him forever.

Until that day, may our lives reflect the light of His presence. Let every word we speak and every act of love we show point others to the One who came near. The story that began in Bethlehem continues in us as we carry His truth, His grace, and His glory into the world.

Here are a few final reflections to encourage your heart as we conclude this devotional journey:

Let Christ Dwell Richly Within You

The same Word who became flesh still lives in you through the Holy Spirit. Nurture His presence daily through prayer, worship, and the Word.

Reflect His Light Wherever You Go

Just as the manger shone with God's glory, your life can shine with His love. Be a beacon of grace and truth in a world that desperately needs His hope.

Live in Daily Gratitude for the Savior

Christmas may come once a year, but its meaning lasts forever. Let gratitude for Christ's coming shape every season of your life.

Share the Story of Redemption

The story didn't end in Bethlehem, it continues through you. Tell others of the Savior who came near so they too may know His life and love.

Keep Your Eyes on the Promise of Eternity

The Child in the manger is the King who will return in glory. Live faithfully and expectantly, knowing that one day you will dwell with Him forever.

Supportive Scriptures

Exodus 25:8 *And let them make me a sanctuary; that I may dwell among them.* **(The Old Testament foreshadowing of God dwelling among His people fulfilled in Christ.)**

John 1:1-3 *In the beginning was the Word, and the Word was with God, and the Word was God. The same was in the beginning* *with God. All things were made by him; and without him was not anything made that was made.* **(Shows the eternal divinity of Christ before His incarnation.)**

Prayer

Lord Jesus, thank You for coming to dwell among us. Thank You for revealing Your glory, full of grace and truth. As I leave this season of reflection, may I carry Christmas in my heart every day, living in Your presence. Amen.

Reflection Question

How will you carry the truth of "God with us" into the new year ahead?

The story of Christmas doesn't end at the manger it lives on in every heart where Christ reigns.

Notes

Closing Prayer

The Light Has Come

Message

As this 30-day journey draws to a close, we stand in awe of the faithfulness of God. From the first whisper of promise to the radiant fulfillment in Christ, His light has never faded. It has pierced the darkness, filled the waiting, and revealed a Savior who still dwells among us.

The same Light that shone over Bethlehem now lives within every believer. We carry it into the world not as a flicker of hope, but as a flame sustained by grace. The journey does not end here; it continues each day we choose to walk in His truth and reflect His glory.

May every promise you've read and every truth you've embraced remind you that God's Word never returns void. The Light has come and that Light still shines through you.

Prayer of Gratitude

Heavenly Father,

Thank You for the gift of Your Son, the true Light of the world. Thank You for fulfilling every promise spoken and for shining hope into our hearts through Jesus Christ.

As I close this devotional, let Your Word continue to dwell richly within me. May the light of Christ guide my steps, warm my spirit, and lead me in paths of righteousness. Help me to carry His presence into my home, my work, and every corner of my life.

When I grow weary, remind me of the manger that held majesty. When I feel lost, remind me that Your light still leads the way. And when I rejoice, may my praise rise like the song of angels declaring that the Savior has come, and His glory fills the earth.

Thank You, Lord, for the Light that never fades.
In Jesus' name, **Amen.**

About the Author

Nadia A. L. Farrington is a devoted writer, teacher, and faith-builder with a heart to illuminate God's Word for everyday believers. Through her brand *Whispers at Sunrise*, she creates devotionals, prayer journals, Bible study guides, and faith-based digital resources that help readers draw closer to Christ one quiet moment at a time.

Nadia's passion for writing grew out of her own journey of seeking God, where she discovered that even the softest whisper from His presence can transform a life. Her work reflects a gentle blend of biblical depth, encouragement, and practical guidance, making spiritual growth both accessible and deeply personal.

She is committed to helping believers understand Scripture, cultivate a lifestyle of prayer, and walk confidently in their God-given purpose. Whether through her devotionals, online courses, or guided journals, Nadia writes with a clear mission: **to point hearts back to Jesus, the true Light who leads us from promise to fulfillment.**

When she's not writing, Nadia enjoys creating peaceful devotional spaces, crafting guided prayer experiences, and encouraging others to remain steadfast in their calling. Her desire is that every reader encounters God's love, truth, and presence in a way that brings lasting transformation.

Closing Scripture and Charge

Till I come, give attendance to reading, to exhortation, to doctrine. Neglect not the gift that is in thee, which was given thee by prophecy, with the laying on of the hands of the presbytery.

— 1 Timothy 4:13–14

As this devotional journey comes to a close, let this scripture be the final word that rests upon your heart.
A reminder.
A commissioning.
A personal call from God.

Paul's words to Timothy echo through time, landing gently yet powerfully in the lives of every believer who desires to walk faithfully with Christ. These verses are more than instruction they are invitation. They pull us back to the foundation of spiritual growth: **the Word, encouragement, teaching,** and **the faithful stewardship of the gift God placed within us**.

You, too, have been entrusted with something holy a gift, a calling, a purpose that God Himself planted within you. Do not neglect it. Do not minimize it. Do not silence it. Nurture it. Guard it. Use it boldly for His glory.

Let this be your charge as you step beyond these pages:

- **Continue in the Word.**

- **Encourage those around you.**

- **Hold fast to sound teaching.**

- **Honor the gift God breathed into you.**

May this scripture guide your heart long after this devotional is finished, reminding you that God has called, equipped, and appointed you for such a time as this.